Dear God, Hear My Cry

Prayers for Urban Teens

Lisa D. Williams

04 05 06 07 08 09 10 11 12 13—10 9 8 7 6 5 4 3 2 1

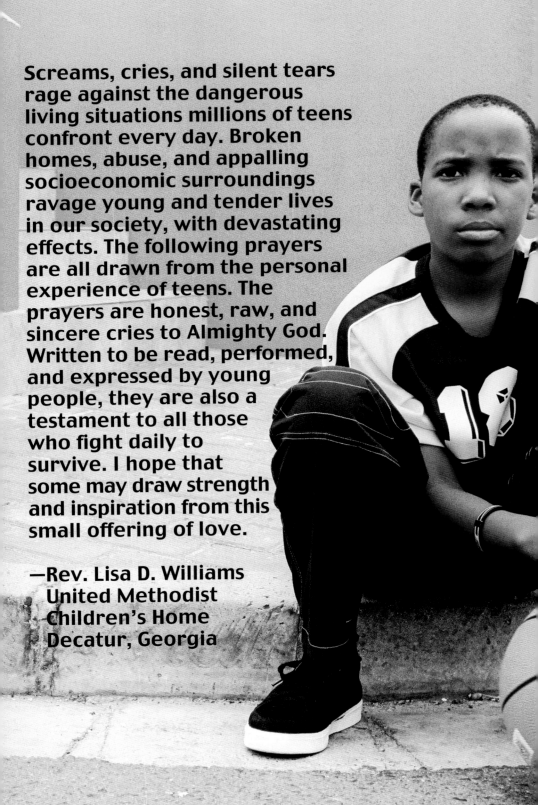

Screams, cries, and silent tears rage against the dangerous living situations millions of teens confront every day. Broken homes, abuse, and appalling socioeconomic surroundings ravage young and tender lives in our society, with devastating effects. The following prayers are all drawn from the personal experience of teens. The prayers are honest, raw, and sincere cries to Almighty God. Written to be read, performed, and expressed by young people, they are also a testament to all those who fight daily to survive. I hope that some may draw strength and inspiration from this small offering of love.

—Rev. Lisa D. Williams
United Methodist
Children's Home
Decatur, Georgia

Dedicated to my sweet baby, Nicholas, who left early
to be with God

JUST FOR YOU,

NICHOLAS EDWARD WILLIAMS (N.E.W.)

Nicholas Edward Williams was our brother.
We loved him like no other.

We can't believe he died at the age of two.
Nicholas, this is just for you.

At the funeral, they said he acted like a grown man.
Now he's in heaven, holding God's hand.

People say he was too young to die.
We walk around, daily asking why?

Won't somebody tell us why he had to go?
Why? For we just don't know.

Nick, you are living in heavenly grace,
Eating ravioli, with a smile on your face.

Your life was precious, more precious than gold.
That's why this story has to be told.

Nick's seventy brothers and sisters in this children's
    home
Will always remember him now that he's gone.

Though we wonder why he went away
And on this earth we had to stay,

We know he's with mighty God on high
So we'll never have to say goodbye.

(by DeAngelo Smith, Rickey Woolf, and James Garrett)

BEGINNINGS

Dear God,
A soul is born into this world—
Be it a boy or even a girl.
Created precious by God for life,
Developed with love amidst the world's strife,
Eventually this child will learn and grow,
Forgiving and trusting, taking life slow.
Given now this youth, this gift of love,
Help him with teachings that come from above.
Introduce her early to seeking God's way,
Just help them to believe there will be better days.
Kindness offered to all persons they know,
Let every teen show love for their friend and for their foe.
Make their minds strive to study God's Word,
Not just to wait till it's something they've heard.
Open their minds to receive suggestions.
Please allow them to ask, indeed, many questions.
Quick always to lend a helping hand, teach them to
Respect every woman and man.
Singing songs to God, with hands upraised,
To you, oh Lord, we lift our hearts in praise.
Ungrateful our teens shall never be.
Verbal teachings will also help them to see,
With Christ in their lives to help them do right—
X-tra time with the Lord—they shall not fight.
Young, full of joy, each youth can grow.
Zealous to walk on God's path, they'll go.

Amen

(For teens attempting to reconcile painful situations)

Dear God,

How can I accept my life?

It seems a cruel blow from an all-powerful God.

What happened when you were giving out families?

Why did I get such a bad deal?

Here I am, lost in the world,

Shuffled to and fro,

Unwanted, unloved; and where are you?

If you are real, please help me.

There is nowhere else to turn;

I can't run away.

Look at me: I am tormented and alone.

Help me, Lord.

Amen.

(Inspired by and dedicated to all the precious
youth struggling to find their way)

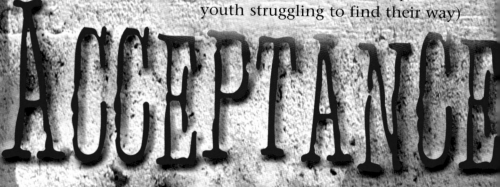

ACCEPTANCE

BLESSINGS

(For teens acknowledging all the good things in life)

Dear God,

Blessings are special.

Blessings are wonderful.

Lord, please allow your blessings to be found daily in our lives.

Blessings remind us of your love.

Help us also to joyfully receive these blessings.

God, you have given us the blessings of life, food, family,
   and more.

You love us so much—words cannot express.

Blessings can come in the form of rap CDs, brand-name clothes,
   or even a radio.

Remind us to always thank you for our wonderful blessings!

If we don't, we should!

Amen.

(Inspired by Meagan, age 13)

CHILDREN ARE SPECIAL

(For teens learning to appreciate their childhood)

Dear God,
Children are awesome!
Children are SO awesome.
Children bring much laughter and
  play into our lives.
Children are full of happiness, love,
  and joy.
Children enhance life experiences.
Children see abundant possibilities
  in things.
Children rekindle our dreams.
Children can grow into teens
  who are still joyful, still hopeful,
  still believing.
Amen.

(By Anne Henry)

Do Unto Others

(For teens struggling to find God's love in the midst of abuse)

Dear God,

"Do unto others" is the Golden Rule,
But how does this help?
My sisters and I can't find any food.

"Do unto others," I heard pastor preach,
But where was he last night
When we cried from being beaten?

"Do unto others," it has been said.
Yet where were you, Lord,
As our bruises turned purple and red?

"Do unto others" comes straight
    from above.
Help us to be safe, Lord, as we search
For your love.

Amen.

(Inspired by Marie, age 12)

EVIL

(For teens learning to overcome evil in their lives)

Dear God,

Evil is when someone kills.
Evil happens when temptations come.
Evil often bears gifts of sorrow,
    destruction, and sad songs.
Evil seeks to destroy good people.
Evil even hurt you, Lord Jesus Christ,
    by nailing you to a wooden tree.
Evil uses the weapons of
    discouragement and despair.
Evil can be fought by praying the
    Lord's Prayer.
Amen.

(Inspired by Christian, age 10)

FINALLY FIGURED IT OUT

(For teens working to develop positive self-esteem)

Dear God,

Finally figured it out what I'm good at.
I'm a poet with confidence, and that's a fact!

I'll make it in this world—this I believe.
The word *can't* is a serious pet peeve.

One thing I've learned, though, is life is not fair.
There are dangers to face, and of evil we must
    beware.

My life is not perfect—that part is true.
But I am learning more and more how to put my
    trust in you.

That's why I'm special; that's why I've grown.
With you, Lord, in my life, I can make it on my own.
Amen.

(Inspired by Katrina, age 17)

GRANDSON'S PRAYER

(A LITTLE G'S PRAYER)
(For teens trying to escape street life)

Heavenly Father, please hear me tonight.
I need so much guidance just to live my life right.
Sometimes the pressure is so hard to bear.
I often wonder if anyone cares.
How can I wake up and face a new day,
Knowing I have to live my life this crazy way?
Heavenly Father, forgive all my sins.
I want to change. Where do I begin?
Give me the strength to resist this wild life I desire.
Help me to escape from nightly gunfire.
God help my family whose eyes silently plead
For me not to go out as they all watch me leave.
And God bless my grandma, who cries every night,
Worrying whether I'll be killed in a deadly gunfight.
Heavenly Father, answer my prayer.
Please let me know that you're listening up there.
When will it end? And what's it all for?
To prove to my "homies" I'm down, I'm hardcore?
At times I wonder how I will die—
Bullet in my back or knife in my side?
Heavenly Father, please hear me tonight.
Give me the courage to live my life right.
Show me the way Lord, show me the light.
Give my heart peace so I won't have to fight.
Thanks for forgiveness and for being there.
And Lord, thank you for listening to a little G's prayer.
Amen.

(Inspired by Caesar, age 19)

Hide Me Behind the Cross

(For teens striving to be more like Christ)

Dear God,

Hide me behind the cross.
Let Christ be seen, not me.
Let me proclaim God's Precious Word
For all eternity.

   Hide me behind the cross.
   Let Christ be seen, not me.
   If we would only follow the examples
     of Christ,
   There would be no me, but we.

Hide me behind the cross
Let Christ be seen, not me.
If Christ were placed for all to see,
He would get the Victory.

   Hide me behind the cross.
   Let Christ be seen, not me.
   When Christ's love shines for all to see,
   Then surely the enemy would flee.

Hide me behind the cross,
Let Christ be seen, not me.
When we love as Christ loves us,
What a wonderful world this will be!

(Inspired by youth seeking fiath despite their struggles)

Innocence

(For teens struggling with the effects
of sexual abuse)

Dear God,
My innocence was taken from me at a very
    young early age.
I had to grow up before I was able to fully
    understand
Who I am and why you made me.
Why was I denied the chance to just be a kid?
Why was I denied the opportunity to laugh,
    sing, jump rope, ride skates, or play with
    dolls?
I've seen and done more in my short time here
    on earth
Than many adults will experience in a lifetime.
Why?
Someone took away the most precious gift you
    gave me:
Innocence.
Amen.

(Inspired by Tara, age 14)

Joy

(FOR TEENS LEARNING TO FIND JOY
IN EVERYDAY THINGS)

DEAR GOD,

WITH JOY COMES LOVE—
LOVE FOR A BIRD THAT FLIES HIGH
IN THE SKY.

WITH JOY COMES PEACE—
PEACE CAN BE FOUND AT JESUS'
FEET.

WITH JOY COMES WONDER—
WONDER IS REVEALED IN GOD'S
BEAUTIFUL CREATION.

WITH JOY COMES FAITH—
FAITH SHINES FROM THE MOMENT WE
ARE BORN.

I CAN FIND JOY IN MY HEART, TOO.
AMEN.

(INSPIRED BY TONYA, AGE 11)

Keep Holding On

(FOR TEENS WHO ARE BECOMING FAITH WARRIORS)

WHEN YOU FEEL LIKE GIVING UP,
    KEEP HOLDING ON!
WHEN YOU FEEL AS THOUGH NOBODY
CARES,
    KEEP HOLDING ON!
WHEN YOU FEEL MISUNDERSTOOD,
    KEEP HOLDING ON!
WHEN YOU FEEL UNLOVED,
    KEEP HOLDING ON!
WHEN YOU FEEL LIKE YOU'RE LOSING
YOUR MIND,
    KEEP HOLDING ON!
WHEN ALL ELSE FAILS,
REMEMBER GOD NEVER FAILS.
STAY IN THE LORD AND
    KEEP HOLDING ON!
AMEN.

(INSPIRED BY KEVIN, AGE 11)

Love

(For teens who are looking for encouragement in God's love)

Dear God,
    Love takes away all hurt and pain.
Love is the sunshine that comes after rain.
    Love is a hug as you greet a friend.
Love is a strong feeling that will never end.
    Love is a cheerleader when life's full of doubt.
Love helps you hold on when grief makes you shout.
    Love is the happiness found in a smile.
Love pulls you forward when family's been gone
        awhile.
    Love soothes all anger when you're really mad.
Love peps up your step and makes you feel glad.
Amen.

(Inspired by Bobby, age 15)

MY PRESENT VS. MY PAST

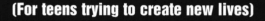

(For teens trying to create new lives)

Dear God,
Living is hard for me.
    I miss my old life but don't want
    to turn back.
Before, I was gang banging and
trying to make ends meet.
    My gang members were my
    family.
My life was falling apart.
    I could have stopped it, but didn't
    know where to start.
Instead, I just acted all thuggish
while failing school,
    And experimenting with drugs
    because I thought it was cool.
Now I'm catching up with my
grades, trying not to act like a fool.
    I need an education. I've already
    got a man.
I'm making right decisions. Can I
make it toward my exit?
    If you help me, Lord, I can!
Amen.

(Inspired by Kate, age 16)

Nobody Understands

(For teens struggling with the reality of abandonment)

Dear God,
When she had nothing to gain but hate,
   All a single teenager could do was wait.
She is alone searching for love and hope in a friend.
   Her strength is gone; she just wants her storm to end.
She's been struggling, trying to find someone to care,
   Her problems are too much for just one person to bear.
She's been singing to be free, trying to understand what
     she sees.
   At every turn is violence and shooting, killing, stealing,
     and thug's drug dealing.
She has nowhere to go, she has nothing to do,
   And she wonders why NO ONE UNDERSTANDS
     what she is going through.
She reaches out to others in spite of the drugs.
   Still so young, all she wants is a little love.
With the odds against her, will a future be found?
   She feels nothing but fear and dread all around.
She can only dream of a family's loving arms,
   living off the streets, free from all hurt and harm.
But life remains torture and she continues to fall,
   Living without happiness is the hardest of all.
Is there a future, will her life soon go on?
   Maybe not, it seems that her teen years are gone.
Amen.

(Inspired by Christina, age 14)

On My Own

(For teens who have not had a home)

Dear God,
I've been on my own for a very long time.
Why I had to leave home still lays heavy
   on my mind.

The mean urban streets are really no joke.
I've met some nice people and some crazy folk.

Making ends meet was hard at first.
Believe me, before it gets better, it will
   get worse.

I've got to make a change, to overcome.
The race is not given to the swift, but
   to those who steadily run.

I've got to survive as a young black man dealing
   with strife
In this dog-eat-dog game called "life."

Amen.

(Inspired by Anthony, age 17)

PROMISES PROMISES

(For teens coping with rejection)

Dear God,
Promises, promises—I heard it all before.
   My parents said we'd be together as a
   family, but then they walked out the door.
Promises, promises—keep your words
    to yourself.
   My heart has been broken over and over
   Then put aside and placed on a shelf.
Promises, promises—be careful what you say.
   For your unmet promises might come back
    to haunt you one day.
Promises, promises—I thought this world had
    gone wrong
   When I was deserted and left in the streets,
   afraid and alone.
Promises, promises—there is only one man
    who holds my hand.
   His name is Jesus, and he helps me when
    I can't stand.
Promises, promises—maybe you should meet
    him too.
   Perhaps you'll let him offer the kind of love
    you never really knew.
Amen.

(Inspired by Joy, age 8)

Quick to Love

(For teens who are searching for love)

Dear God,
You inspire so many kids; and
    in our eyes, You're number one.
You love with great wisdom shining
    through all you've done.
You pick us up when we are down.
Your voice is sweet, a heavenly
    sound.
You are the one we all look up to.
You touch a young person's life
    in all that you do.
You are there for us when our tears
    begin to fall.
You are the God we serve and always
    give your all.
You are the one who helps to get us
    through,
To You we say thanks for just
    being You.
Amen.

(Inspired by all the kids whose
lives are a beautiful testimony)

REAL FORGIVENESS

(For teens learning how to forgive those who have wronged them)

Dear God,
Let's get real about forgiving others, shall we?
We say, "I'll forgive . . . but I'll never forget."
Real forgiveness looks past the act that was done
and reaches out in love, forgetting and
forgiving those who have wronged you.

If we say we love God yet we choose not to forgive,
how then can we say we **REALLY** love?
It takes a strong person to forgive persons for the
wrongs they have done.

Help us to love like you, Lord, and to forget and
forgive
the way you forgive.
As often as a person needs our forgiveness,
they need our love.

Amen.

(Inspired by Tiffany, age 15)

Smile

(For teens who, despite all obstacles, are basking in hope)

Dear God,

No matter how cold it is outside,

No matter how much ice or snow,

I stay warm in the glow of a smile.

Wherever we may go,

No matter the heat of the burning sun,

No matter the raging fire,

I hold on to your sweet, sweet love

And call you every hour.

Amen.

(Inspired by Nicole, age 9)

TEARS

(For teens experiencing grief)

When I pray,
I like to talk to my grandma.

Tears fall when memories come to view
The days and weeks we shared alone, just me and you.
   You were my best friend.
   I'll never forget how you rescued me from abuse
      so many times.
   You were the sun in my day;
   You were brisk winds to make the flowers sway.
At only age 80, you left me; you passed away.
My tears come.
How do you stop tears that don't understand?
Why did you, my only help, my only refuge, have to go?
   You opened my heart to show me who I was inside.
   You always told the truth, leaving nothing in disguise.
   You told me to be strong when I felt all hope was gone.
These past two years have been so hard with nothing left to gain.
I guess these tears I cry each day come from love, not pain.
   If only I could have said goodbye to let you know how much I cared.
   Even though you are in heaven, I'll never forget the love we shared.
Amen.

(Inspired by Christina, age 15)

UNCONDITIONAL LOVE

(FOR TEENS LEARNING MORE ABOUT GOD'S LOVE)

DEAR GOD,

UNCONDITIONAL LOVE COMES FROM YOU,
  FROM ABOVE.
IT'S THE KIND OF LOVE WE NEED PLENTY OF.

UNCONDITIONAL LOVE LASTS FOREVER
  MORE.
IT GOES TO INFINITY AND RIGHT TO THE
  CORE.

UNCONDITIONAL LOVE HAS NO
  ATTACHMENTS OR STRINGS.
THIS KIND OF LOVE CAN BE GIVEN TO
  SOMEONE OR SOMETHING.

UNCONDITIONAL LOVE MUST BE SOUGHT,
REGARDLESS OF THOSE WHO THINK IT
  CAN BE BOUGHT.

UNCONDITIONAL LOVE MUST BE
  CHERISHED BY THOSE WHO RECEIVE IT.
WE NEVER REALLY KNOW JUST WHEN
  WE'LL NEED IT.

AMEN.

(INSPIRED BY STACEY, AGE 13)

Very Alone,
Very Afraid

(For teens facing isolation)

Dear God,

Very alone, very afraid.
When will this nightmare end?
Very alone, very afraid.
I thought You were my friend!

Very alone, very afraid.
I want to be loved in this cold, cruel world.
Very alone, very afraid.
Me, am I a lovable girl?

Very alone, very afraid.
Help me, God, not to feel this way.
Very alone, very afraid.
Could I perhaps see a brighter day?

Amen.

(Inspired by Rachel, age 8)

WHAT REALLY COUNTS

(FOR TEENS ENCOUNTERING RACISM AND PREJUDICE)

DEAR GOD,

THE COLOR OF MY SKIN IS WHITE.
THE MAKE-UP OF MY BLOOD IS MIXED.
THE CONTENT OF MY HEART IS GOLD.
THE SHAPE OF MY BODY IS BODACIOUS
    AND BOLD.

I'VE OVERCOME THE POWER OF HATE.
THERE IS A BETTER LIFE FOR ME—
    IT'S NOT TOO LATE.
FOR INSIDE, I'M TRUE AND GOOD.
IT'S ONLY OTHER PEOPLE WHO THINK
    I'M MISUNDERSTOOD.

DESPITE WHAT OTHERS DO AND SAY,
I AM BEAUTIFUL; THIS I CAN CONVEY!
WITH GOD, IT'S NEITHER BLACK NOR
    WHITE—
ONLY PEACE, PURE LOVE, AND RADIANT
    LIGHT.

AMEN.

(INSPIRED BY MICHELLE, AGE 15)

x-tra time

(For teens fighting to avoid death in the streets)

Dear God,

I pray for X-tra time—
X-tra time to make up my mind
Concerning life, goals, and dreams.

I pray for X-tra time—
X-tra time to make up my mind
To seek your guidance as I strive for my goal.

I pray for X-tra time—
X-tra time to leave a positive mark
On someone else's life.

I pray for X-tra time—
X-tra time to live and not be a statistic,
To overcome the trials and make a difference.

Lord, I pray for X-tra time.
There is enough pain and hurt in this world
Without my adding to the strife.

Amen.

(Inspired by Jeremy, age 15)

You Know Sorrow

(For teens suffering with depression)

Dear God,

The darkness surrounds me and blinds my way.
The pain violently hits me like a runaway train.
How could I have been so stupid, so wrong?
How could I have hurt you for so long?

The fear that freezes the blood in my veins,
The fear of losing the one thing I cannot claim,
The shame that I feel burns right through me.
It eats at my soul, and I just want to flee.

Sorrow for my actions fills my mind.
Placing blame after blame is just a waste of time.
Your words seem distant, indifferent, and cold.
Years of abuse, I was forced to behold.

Shame eating through me,
Sorrow choking the air I breathe,
Fear freezing my blood—
Sorrow is all that I can feel.

Amen.

(Inspired by Natalie, age 15)

Z ANSWER is YOU

(For teens asking the ultimate question about life)

Heavenly God,

Z-answer is you, Lord.
You gave me the courage
When I was beaten and bruised,
Misused and discouraged.

Z-answer was right here inside me
All along.
When I was afraid and lonely,
I didn't know how to be strong.

Z-answer to all the questions,
To my why, why, why?
Is answered by you, Lord.
You didn't put me here to cry.

Z-answer to the hatred, the sickness,
And the pain,
Was found in the morning sun,
After evening rain.

Z-answer to the despair, when I
Just wanted to die,
Remains in your loving care,
For your love does not lie.

Z-answer that kept me safe
Both night and day
Was deep down within me.
All I needed to do was PRAY.

Amen.

(Inspired by Corey, age 12)

ENDINGS

Why should I pray?
      This is the question that troubles my day.
Why would I pray,
      Lord, when I can't even get away?

I've prayed to God to end my pain,
      to repair my scars, to end this rain.
I've prayed to God to come see about me,
      to stop this violence, to let me flee.

Hear my cry, God.
      Let me know that You are there.
Hear my cry, God,
      in my moment of despair.

You've heard my cry, God.
      I thank You for what You have done.
You've heard my cry, God.
      I want to live so others will see
        that You're my number 1.

Lisa Williams